WILDFLOWERS

WILDFLOWERS

A GUIDE TO
FAMILIAR AMERICAN FLOWERS
a Golden Guide® from St. Martin's Press

by
HERBERT S. ZIM
and
ALEXANDER C. MARTIN
Former Senior Biologist, U.S. Fish and Wildlife Service

Illustrated by
RUDOLF FREUND

Revised by
JONATHAN P. LATIMER and KAREN STRAY NOLTING
with
DR. ROBERT A. DEFILIPPS
National Museum of Natural History
Smithsonian Institution

St. Martin's Press 🐾 New York

A Golden Guide® is a registered trademark of Golden Books Publishing Company, Inc., used under license.

ISBN 1-58238-162-3

First published under the title *Flowers*

FOREWORD

For more than a generation this book, along with other Golden Guides, has introduced thousands of children and adults to the diversity of the natural world. It has helped increase people's awareness of the environment and add to their pleasure in learning about and understanding nature. This guide illustrates more than two hundred of the most common and most widely distributed wildflowers found in North America. The text gives concise information to help identify each, as well as other wildflowers in the same family.

The flowers in this guide were carefully selected from the thousands of varieties found growing wild in North America. The development of the first edition relied on the assistance of many experts, including Neil Hotchkiss, Francis Uhler, and A. L. Nelson of the U.S. Fish and Wildlife Service, and P. L. Ricker of the Wild Flower Preservation Society. Invaluable contributions were also made by Frank C. McKeever, Carol H. Woodward, Elizabeth Hall, and Elizabeth McConnell of the New York Botanical Garden. James L. Luteyn, Curator, The New York Botanical Garden, advised on a later revision.

The organizing and writing abilities of Herbert S. Zim, who conceived Golden Guides, and Alexander C. Martin have proven their excellence. The artistic skills of Rudolf Freund did much to assure this guide's success. This revision was guided by the comments of Dr. Robert A. DeFilipps of the National Museum of Natural History, Smithsonian Institution and David Challinor, Scientist Emeritus, Smithsonian Institution. It reflects the latest information on wildflowers. We hope it will continue to help readers of all ages recognize and appreciate the wildflowers around us.

J.P.L.
K.S.N.

HOW TO USE THIS BOOK

You can use this book better if you know the unique features in it. In the first place, the flowers are arranged in four groups, according to color, as shown on the color chart below.

Color of Flower   **Color of Tab**

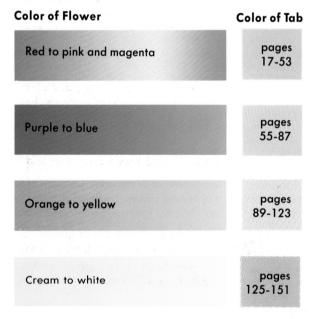

Color of Flower	Color of Tab
Red to pink and magenta	pages 17-53
Purple to blue	pages 55-87
Orange to yellow	pages 89-123
Cream to white	pages 125-151

Many wildflowers, such as the Asters, Columbines, and Morning-glories, occur in several colors. These have been put with the color that is most common, though several shades may be illustrated on the same plate. At the end of each color section are listed wildflowers which have not been included, even though some are of that color. These will be found under their predominating color in another section.

To help beginners know wildflowers, the plants are presented mainly in groups (or genera), rather than by kinds (or species). You may thus see a group of Gentians, Asters, Violets, or Sunflowers at a glance. Note the similarities within each group as well as the diversities in color and form. These points enable you to recognize flowers that are not illustrated. By selecting important genera this book is able to present many types of flowers which grow widely over our country. However, some species which are very common, very important, or have no close relatives have been treated separately.

The color of a flower is your key in using this book. But keep in mind that shades of color vary among different species of the same genus, and even among plants of the same species. A flower you have found may be of a different color from the one illustrated. But the form of the flower and the general field appearance of the plant should help you.

Thumb through this book at odd moments and you will soon be familiar enough with flowers to recognize some of them at sight. You may even be able to identify the plants by their general form, their habit of growth, or the shape of the leaves before the flowers have opened.

When you start to identify an unknown plant, look at the range maps first. They will indicate whether the

150 species

flowers illustrated on that page occur where you have found your specimen. On some maps, a deeper tint of the color (as on the sample map here) indicates a greater abundance of plants are found in that area. Even within the broad limits of their known ranges plants vary. Some are restricted to woodlands, meadows, swamps, roadsides, or where favorable conditions prevail. Others, the so-called "weeds," have adapted to less favorable or more generalized conditions.

In your rambles you may find rare plants that are not in the book at all. You may then want to use more advanced books or perhaps seek the aid of an expert. To remember the names of the plants you have found and identified, keep a record of those you see. (The last page of the book can be used for this purpose.) Note the date and place where your specimen was found. Your record will be a quick reference for you to use again and again.

As you learn more about wildflowers, knowledge of their scientific names grows increasingly useful. The scientific names of the wildflowers illustrated in this book are given on pages 153-155.

SEEING FLOWERS

WHERE TO LOOK Wildflowers grow almost everywhere. You'll find them in deserts, swamps, and fields, on mountains, roadsides, and city lots—in all parts of our country. From the window of an express train tearing through New York suburbs on a July morning, 27 kinds were seen in a half-hour. On a short country walk you can see twice as many. And if that walk takes you along a meadow, past a marsh, through woods, and by a beach, more kinds of plants will be seen than on any single type of land, no matter how picturesque.

Flowers are in bloom every month of the year in some part of this country. Only a few are found during the winter, when most plants are resting, but spring is barely under way before flowers are out. Some push up through snow. Many bloom before their leaves are out. A general rush of blooming comes later in the spring, followed by a slackening in early summer and a final splurge in late summer and early fall. This pattern varies from place to place. Mountain and desert wildflowers have shorter, more brilliant seasons. Field and wayside plants are more conspicuous in the fall. In this book the season of blooming is given for every plant.

WHAT TO SEE Flowers are far more intriguing than many people suspect. A flower is more than a splash of color and a design. Each part of a flower usually has a task to perform, and the whole flower has the essential job of reproducing the plant. So the detailed floral parts may prove fascinating once you get to know them. Flowers

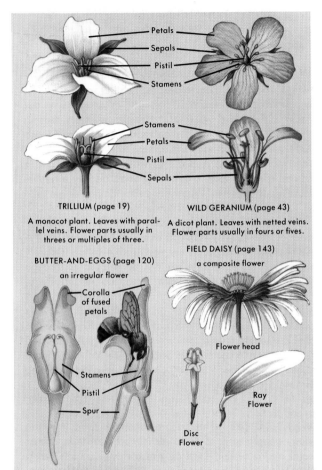

Petals
Sepals
Pistil
Stamens

Stamens
Petals
Pistil
Sepals

TRILLIUM (page 19)

A monocot plant. Leaves with parallel veins. Flower parts usually in threes or multiples of three.

WILD GERANIUM (page 43)

A dicot plant. Leaves with netted veins. Flower parts usually in fours or fives.

FIELD DAISY (page 143)

a composite flower

BUTTER-AND-EGGS (page 120)

an irregular flower

Corolla of fused petals

Stamens
Pistil
Spur

Flower head

Disc Flower

Ray Flower

PARTS OF DIFFERENT FLOWER TYPES

have but one goal—producing seed—but they do not all go about it the same way. Some spread their pollen by wind. Others attract and even trap insects to perform this essential function. The special floral structures developed in different plant groups have made flowers as varied and as distinctively beautiful as they are. Look closely. These structures are worth seeing.

Flowers have much in common despite differences in appearance. The essential parts of every flower are the pistils (female parts) and the stamens (male parts). The stamens produce pollen grains which, through fertilization, enable the ovules in the pistil to develop into seeds. Around these basic organs, flowers usually have a ring of showy petals, the attractive part of the flower we see first. The sepals are a ring of smaller, generally green bracts below the petals. The pattern of these parts varies. Sometimes the petals are fused into a tube; sometimes the sepals are colored. Variations in the number and arrangement of pistils and stamens, plus the color and shape of the petals and sepals, help us identify the different flowers.

FLOWERS AND WEEDS   A flower is, of course, only one part of a plant. But we also use the word loosely to mean a flowering plant. Many flowering plants are important to us, providing materials for food, clothing, and shelter. Other kinds flourish where we don't want them, competing with cultivated plants. We call these "weeds." Most weeds are active, hardy flowering plants that thrive in poor soil and under adverse conditions. Some weeds have small, inconspicuous flowers and may produce many seeds. Weeds are worth knowing. Some are good to eat. Even if they are not very attractive, they are likely to be important plants.

WILDFLOWER CONSERVATION　Wildflowers are one of our nation's irreplaceable assets. They have but limited economic value—no fortunes have been made in them. But attractive, showy flowers offer us a kind of enjoyment afforded by few other things in nature. As with other natural resources, we once thought flowers to be unlimited. Now we know better. In some areas, especially near large cities, wildflowers have been over-picked. Some kinds have completely disappeared from places where they once were common. Trailing Arbutus, Fringed Gentians, and a number of Lilies and Orchids are seldom seen nowadays. Wildflowers are the kind of resource we do not miss till they are gone. And then regret does no good.

Learn to enjoy flowers where they grow and learn to leave them for others to enjoy, too. Do not pick them in parks or other protected areas. If you do want to pick one for study, be sure that others are growing in the vicinity of the one you have spotted. If the places they grow are not disturbed, wildflowers will reseed the area, or will continue to spread by underground stems or bulbs. As long as you realize that the enjoyment of flowers is something to be shared with others, our wildflowers will be safe.

AMATEUR ACTIVITIES

The best way to enjoy wildflowers is to observe them and study them right where they are growing. Beginners can learn more from an hour with live flowers than from a day with dead, dried ones.

When you look at a flowering plant, look for details of the flower, fruit, stem, and leaves. Use a magnifying glass. The more you look, the more you will see, and the more interesting flowers will become. See where the plant is growing and what other plants grow with it.

After you know some of the more common wildflowers, turn your attention to their relatives. Find different members of the Pea or of the Composite families and note how similar is the flower pattern within a plant group. Looking at wildflowers will always be enjoyable, but after a while you may want to do more.

PHOTOGRAPHING FLOWERS Most flowers can be easily photographed with a camera and a close-up lens attachment. The close-up lens makes it possible to come within a foot or two of the flower and still stay in focus. Practice first on large meadow or roadside flowers, like the Daisy, Sunflower, or Milkweed. After you have had some success, try smaller flowers and woodland plants that grow in the shade. For these a tripod and a flash attachment may be necessary. Color film makes it possible for the amateur to get striking pictures of flowers to enjoy all winter.

GROWING WILDFLOWERS Cultivated flowers have been developed from wild species that may also grow in gardens. A wildflower garden can be most attractive and, in addition, it will give you a chance to study flowers at your leisure.

Growing wildflowers does not require much technical skill. Every amateur who makes the effort can succeed. Find out, by observation and reading, the soil and light requirements of the flowers you wish to grow or transplant. If possible, take some soil with them when transplanting. Unless conditions are kept very much the same, the transplants may not thrive. Once a wildflower garden is started, one may even attempt plant breeding and perhaps produce new varieties by crossing or hybridizing, or simply by selecting and planting seeds of the best plants.

USEFUL WILD PLANTS Wild plants were of considerable importance to our forefathers, and many are still used medicinally and as foods. Do you know that Milkweed shoots, Groundnuts, Arrowheads, and Marsh Marigolds are nutritious and tasty? Medicinal plants include Foxgloves (Digitalis), Gentians, and Wintergreen. Other plants worth knowing can be used in teas and tonics. You may wish to find out more about edible, medicinal, and other useful plants—it's knowledge that may be of value in an emergency.

COLLECTING FLOWERS Everyone likes to collect, but too many people start flower collections and too few make collections they can use. Think twice before you start. It's easy to press a dozen or more flowers, but what will that teach you about plants that you couldn't find out by studying them alive? Postpone making a collection till you know the most common flowers in your vicinity and are ready to start a serious study of plants. Remember that if a collector fails to observe, his work is of little value. But if an observer takes notes, they will add immeasurably to the value of his collection.

If you plan to collect, read one of the more advanced books to get help. Locate the materials you need to make a plant press. Don't forget a notebook to keep a record of your specimens. Start with common weeds and practice till you can press flowers without spoiling them. Then go about your collecting systematically, keeping in mind that making a collection does not permit anyone to violate state laws protecting wildflowers.

SPECIAL COLLECTIONS   If you collect, your collection will be a specialized one right from the start. If nothing else, it will be a regional collection—one of local plants. But other special collections are possible. You can collect plants of different habitats: swamp plants, mountain plants, or desert plants. By specializing in some plant community, you can see how plants fit into the life of a seashore or a prairie, or a woodlot. You can pay special attention to plant groups, such as Asters, Goldenrods, or Orchids. Perhaps you may become especially interested in spring flowers or fall flowers.

When you collect flowers, you can also collect fruits, seed pods, or seeds. Many small seeds are curious and attractive when viewed through a magnifying glass. They can be stored in glass vials or cellophane envelopes.

What's more, you can attempt to raise these wildflowers from seed. It may be more difficult than growing Marigolds or Petunias, but the results are much more satisfying.

MORE INFORMATION There are about 20,000 kinds of flowering plants in North America. This guide can offer only a brief introduction to a few of them. Here are a few books and Web sites that you might want to look at as your interest grows:

BOOKS

Craighead, John J., Frank C. Craighead, Jr., and Ray J. Davis, *Rocky Mountain Wildflowers* (Peterson Field Guides), Houghton Mifflin, Boston, 1963.

Cullina, William, *The New England Wild Flower Society Guide to Growing and Propagating Wildflowers*, Houghton Mifflin, Boston, 2000.

Latimer, J. P., and Karen Stray Nolting, *Wildflowers* (Peterson Guides for Young Naturalists), Houghton Mifflin, Boston, 2001.

Newcomb, Lawrence, and Gordon Morrison, *Newcomb's Wildflower Guide*, Little Brown, New York, 1989.

Niehaus, Theodore F., *Pacific States Wildflowers* (Peterson Field Guides), Houghton Mifflin, Boston, 1976.

Niehaus, Theodore F., and Charles L. Ripper, *Southwestern and Texas Wildflowers* (Peterson Field Guides), Houghton Mifflin, Boston, 1984.

Niering, William A., and Nancy C. Olmstead, *North American Wildflowers: Eastern Region* (Audubon Field Guides), Knopf, New York, 1997.

Peterson, Roger Tory, and Margaret McKenny, *A Field Guide to Wildflowers: Northeastern and North-Central North America* (Peterson Field Guides), Houghton Mifflin, Boston, 1996.

Spellenberg, Richard, *North American Wildflowers: Western Region* (Audubon Field Guides), Knopf, New York, 2001.

Venning, Frank D., and Manabu C. Saito, *Wildflowers of North America* (Golden Field Guides), St. Martin's Press, New York, 1984.

WEB SITES

The Internet is full of interesting information about wildflowers. Some keywords to use in searches include native plants and wildflowers. You can also find information by searching for a particular state or type of environment, such as prairie or desert. Some good places to start are:

Lady Bird Johnson Wildflower Center at http://www.wildflower.org/
Wildflower magazine at http://www.wildflowermag.com/
The EPA's wildflower site at http://www.epa.gov/glnpo/greenacres/

CARDINAL FLOWER   This striking plant of rich, moist eastern woodlands and brooksides is the only red Lobelia. Others are blue or white (see page 70). Over-picking has made the Cardinal Flower so rare it now needs protection. When this plant is grown in gardens, hummingbirds often visit its tube-like flowers. Cardinal Flowers grow 2 to 4 feet tall.—*Summer and early fall. Bluebell Family.*

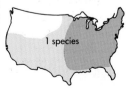

1 species

BEE BALMS These tall, coarse, aromatic mints are also called Wild Bergamot, Oswego Tea, Horsemint. They vary in color from scarlet red to pale lavender. The brilliant red-flowered Oswego Tea grows in moist places, but the other Bee Balms prefer dry waysides and fencerows. Some are native; others, brought from Europe, have gone wild. Indians and early settlers brewed medicinal tea from the leaves.—*Summer and early fall. Mint Family.*

15 species

TRILLIUMS Trilliums are handsome spring plants of moist eastern woodlands and western mountains. As their name implies, they are constructed on a threefold plan: 3 leaves, 3 green sepals, and 3 petals which vary in color from the deep, purple-red of the common Wake-robin through pink to pure white. There are about 42 species—most grow a foot or so high, usually in rich soil. The fruits ripen into reddish or purple berries.—*Spring. Lily Family.*

42 species

GILIAS   About 53 of the 60 kinds of Gilia grow in this country, mainly in western deserts and mountains. Dwarfed species are typical of both these habitats. More commonly, Gilias grow on open slopes and dry hillsides. They are variable and not easily distinguished from one another. All have tubular, funnel- or bell-shaped, 5-petaled flowers. On some the flowers cluster at the top of the plant; in others they scatter along the vertical stem. Gilias vary in color from scarlet to pink, blue, purple, yellow, and white.

Gilias grow from 5 inches to 2 feet tall, with rough or sticky stems. The thin leaves generally alternate along them. The seeds are also sticky when wet. Some are eaten by gamebirds and by desert rodents. One of the best-known Gilias is the Scarlet Gilia or Skyrocket, a plant that covers western hillsides and has a rather disagreeable odor. Other common Gilias include Blue Desert Gilia, Bird's-Eyes, Downy Gilia, and Prickly Gilia.—*Spring to fall. Phlox Family.*

53 species

WILD PINKS These are common in both East and West, especially in fields, open woods, and rocky uplands. They range in color from the scarlet Indian Pink of the Northwest and the crimson Wild Pink of the East to the pink Catchfly and the purple to white Moss Campion of alpine regions. Some are low, branching plants with finely divided, prickly leaves. Others have slender, erect stems.—*Summer and early fall. Pink Family.*

50 species

MORNING-GLORIES This tropical group of some 40-50 species includes the sweet potato. Morning-glories thrive in good soil under a great variety of conditions, especially in the South. The bell-shaped, pleated flowers on twining and trailing, hairy stems, range from scarlet to pink, white, blue, and purple. The large seeds are occasionally eaten by gamebirds.—*Summer and fall. Morning-glory Family.*

40-50 species

CLOVERS Clover grows most abundantly in the East, but 70 of its 85 species are Western. Most of the common kinds have been introduced from Europe. Our honey and bumblebees pollinate the Clovers and help account for their widespread distribution. Clovers grow from 8 inches to 2 feet high in open fields, meadows, lawns, and roadsides. Most have the well-known globular flower-head, made of many tiny, tubular florets, ranging in color from red to pink, yellow, and creamy white. The leaf has 3 leaflets with toothed edges and is marked in

some species with a lighter green triangle on the top. A few western species have as many as 6 or 7 leaflets.

Red, Alsike, and White Clover enrich the soil, are excellent for livestock, and provide our best honey. The small, hard seeds of western Clovers are important foods for quail and other birds. Hop and Bur Clover (page 109) are related to this true Clover group. —*Late spring to early fall. Pea Family.*

85 species

PAINTED-CUPS On prairies and hillsides of the West, a common flower is the brilliant Painted-cup or Indian Paintbrush. The red or yellow stain on the cluster of leaf tips near the flower is characteristic. Painted-cups (100 species) usually grow with erect, bunched stems 12 to 20 inches high. Most are red; some are red and yellow or just yellow. One species is the state flower of Wyoming.—*Spring and summer. Figwort Family.*

100 species

CLARKIAS A number of species of Clarkia are found in meadows, on hillsides, and on mountain slopes throughout the West. One pink-flowered kind is called Farewell-to-spring. The large, 4-petaled flowers, pink to lilac and purple, and the narrow, alternate leaves grow on smooth, branching stems about 2 feet high. Clarkias are showy flowers. Most of them close at night.—*Spring and early summer. Evening Primrose Family.*

35 species

COLUMBINES Columbines—among the most graceful and attractive wildflowers—are found in open woods and mountain meadows. The eastern species is scarlet and yellow. One in the Rockies is blue; another is red. The Blue Columbine—sometimes a very pale blue—is the Colorado state flower. The Northwest has a white-flowered species.

Columbine leaves all have 3 neatly scalloped leaflets. The flowers, each with 5 petals tapering off into a long spur, hang nodding on slender, rigid stalks. They are pollinated by bees and other long-tongued insects. The plants

grow 2 to 3 feet tall. All are perennials, growing anew each year from the underground rootstock. Many garden varieties of Columbines have been developed. The flower matures into an erect, brown capsule containing many black, shiny seeds. Close relatives of Columbines are Monkshood, a western plant with deep blue flowers and a poisonous root, and Larkspur, which bears its blue, purple, or scarlet flowers in long, loose spikes.—*Spring and early summer. Buttercup Family.*

22 species

MALLOWS   This large and widely distributed group of over 100 species ranges in color from scarlet to purple, pink, yellow, and white; in height, from 1 to 6 feet. Some are natives of our western prairies and plains, where they color wide areas. Rose Mallow favors shores and salt marshes. The gay flowers, like miniature Hollyhocks, grow along the slightly hairy stem or in terminal spikes.—*Spring and summer. Mallow Family.*

100 species

RED MAIDS This low, succulent-stemmed plant, also known as Pink Maids and Kisses, is abundant in California and common in neighboring western areas. It prefers cultivated ground, but also grows on hillsides and along the seacoast. The 5-petaled flowers are usually magenta to rose and occasionally white. The small, black, shiny seeds are an important food for western songbirds and rodents.—*Spring. Purslane Family.*

1 species

SHOOTING-STARS The drooping flowers of this plant, with its 5 inverted petals, occur singly or in clusters of 5 at the top of a bare stalk 8 to 20 inches high. The smooth, thickish leaves all grow from the base of the stem. Shooting-stars range in color from red to pink and pale lavender. They are commonly found on moist hillsides, in open woods, and on prairies in the western and middle states. These plants are sometimes cultivated.—*Spring. Primrose Family.*

15 species

FIREWEED As the name implies, Fireweed grows abundantly on burnt-over ground, sometimes blanketing hillsides with pink or lavender blossoms. The widespread Fireweed is common in wooded parts of our Northeast and Northwest. Several related species are mostly smaller and lack showy flowers. The seeds, tufted with white hairs, make the plants look shaggy in the fall, before they scatter.—*Summer. Evening Primrose Family.*

1 species

THISTLES Some native and some European Thistles have become pernicious weeds, crowding fields, pastures, and roadsides. All have the well-known flowerhead, with spiny bracts, leaves, and stem, 1 to 4 feet high. Flowers range from pink to purple, yellow, and white. They are rich in nectar for bees and butterflies. The seeds are eaten by goldfinches, and roots of some species were used as food by Indians.—*Spring and summer. Composite Family.*

60 species

SPIDER FLOWERS These tall, very handsome, somewhat bushy herbs grow in western waste places and along roadsides and river banks. The loose flower clusters in pink, lilac, or yellow are borne at the top of smooth stems 3 to 8 feet high. The seeds form in long, flat pods, which are eaten by wildlife. Spider flowers are sometimes called Bee plant or Skunkweed because of the unpleasant smell of their crushed foliage.— *Spring to early fall. Caper Family.*

9 species

ORCHIDS Orchids are one of the world's largest and most interesting families of plants. But of over 20,000 species only 160 grow in North America. Orchids are highly specialized for insect pollination. One of their 3 petals is modified into a conspicuous "lip," which secretes nectar. This is very noticeable in the Lady-Slippers, those famed pink, white, and yellow Orchids of northern woods. The Showy Lady-Slipper is Minnesota's state flower. The leaves of some Orchids are small; other Orchids have a pair of broad leaves close to the ground. Most grow in rich, moist soil in open woods or in bogs. They run in

color from pink to purple, orange, yellow, and white. A few, in humid parts of the South, and many in the tropics grow on trees, but these airplants are not parasites. Vanilla flavoring is made from the pod of an orchid.

Wild Orchids come up year after year from thick, fleshy roots. They grow slowly, are hard to transplant, and are exceedingly difficult to grow from their very minute seeds. For these reasons Orchids should not be picked.—*Late spring and summer. Orchid Family.*

160 species

SMARTWEEDS About 75 species of Smartweeds thrive along roadsides, in wet meadows, and in marshes. They are spreading weeds, 1 to 4 feet high, with slender clusters of small pink to white flowers. Closely related are such climbing plants as Climbing Buckwheat, Knotweed, and Tearthumbs. The rather large, dark seeds of Smartweeds are choice foods of waterfowl and gamebirds.—*Summer to fall. Buckwheat Family.*

75 species

MEADOW-BEAUTIES The attractive, 4-petaled Meadow-Beauties are natives of wet, grassy flats and sandy pine barrens in the South. The showy, delicate flowers range from pink to lavender to purple, with long, arched, bright yellow stamens. These plants, sometimes called Deergrass, grow 10 to 20 inches high, with squarish stems like Mints. The seeds are in a 4-celled, bur-like capsule.—*Summer. Meadow-Beauty Family.*

10 species

BOUNCING BET   This hardy, widely distributed European Pink, 1 to 2 feet high, thrives along embankments and in other waste places, where it spreads by underground stems. The blooms, with a characteristic spicy odor, are in profuse, flattish clusters. The scalloped petals range from pink to white. When crushed in water, the thick, oval leaves form a lather. Hence another common name —Soapwort.—*Summer and fall. Pink Family.*

1 species

ROSE GENTIANS These delicately fragrant, pink to white, graceful plants grow in moist meadows and savannas, and along the sandy coast—mainly in the Southeast. Some are found in brackish marshes. The Rose Gentians branch often and usually grow 1 to 3 feet high. The large blooms with yellow starlike centers form on slender stalks. The small, symmetrical, opposite leaves have no stalks at all.—*Summer to fall. Gentian Family.*

15 species

FILAREES Filarees are most abundant in the orchards of California and in fields and other open places in the West, where 9 species are known. Only one species occurs in the East, and this sparingly. These cut-leaved, spreading annuals with their Geranium-like flowers are an important food for livestock and wildlife. The name Filaree (Spanish for pin-like) refers to the hard, awl-shaped seeds, which are eaten by many kinds of birds.—*Winter and early spring. Geranium Family.*

9 species

WILD GERANIUMS Of 33 species of Wild Geraniums, about 13 are found in the East and more in the West. They are more closely related to Filarees than to potted Geraniums. Some, like the common Wild Geranium, prefer woodlands. The California Geranium and numerous western species prefer open places. The flowers are 5-petaled; lavender, pink, and white. The plants are loosely branched, with finely cut leaves.—*Spring and early summer. Geranium Family.*

33 species

BEGGARWEEDS The flat, fuzzy "seeds" relished by quail and wild turkey are far more familiar than the flower. They stick tight to clothing during autumn walks in old fields; hence the plants get such names as Sticktights, Tick trefoil, and Tick clover. Of some 160 species,

50 species

50 are found in the United States—mainly in the Southeast. The small, pea-like flowers are magenta, violet, and sometimes white. The wand-like stems grow 1 to 4 feet high.—*Summer and early fall. Pea Family.*

TRAILING ARBUTUS   Trailing Arbutus or Mayflower, state flower of Massachusetts, is cherished as one of the earliest spring flowers. There is only one species in this country. Formerly common in rocky eastern woodlands and sandy soils, Arbutus has become scarce from careless picking. This tough creeper, with coarse, hairy, evergreen leaves, has small pink or white tubular flowers with a spicy fragrance. They are pollinated by flies and bees.—*Late winter to early spring. Heath Family.*

1 species

PURPLE CONEFLOWERS These attractive plants grow in the fields and roadsides of our midland states and are sometimes cultivated. The flowerheads are showy, with long, drooping magenta or purple petals, each notched at the tip. The smooth, sometimes slightly hairy stems are 2 to 4 feet tall. The basal leaves are coarse and sharply toothed; those higher on the stem are smaller, with shallow teeth. — *Early summer to early fall. Composite Family.*

6 species

MILKWORTS   Most Milkworts are tropical. Ours grow mainly in the moist meadows of the Southeast. These dainty plants with small and generally narrow leaves have their purple, pink, orange, or white flowers at the top of slender stems. The blooms may be in compact, Clover-like heads, spikes, or flat-topped clusters, or they may grow singly, as in the small, showy Fringed Milkwort. —*Late spring and summer. Milkwort Family.*

50 species

FLEABANES These plants resemble Asters, but their flowerheads usually have 2 or 3 rows of petal-like rays. Magenta and violet Fleabanes provide vivid splashes of color in alpine meadows of the West. The well-known Daisy Fleabane grows in eastern fields and roadsides. Some of the less showy, pale-flowered species are common weeds of hayfields and fallow ground — 8 inches to over 2 feet high.—*Summer. Composite Family.*

130 species

SPRING BEAUTIES In masses of thousands on river flood plains or in open woods, the frail Spring Beauties, 6 to 12 inches high, make a striking display. The inconspicuous, delicate, pink to white flowers, veined with deeper pink, remain open only in the bright light. These succulent plants have starchy bulbs, which the Indians ate. In the West there are several relatives of the Spring Beauties, all small-flowered too.—*Spring. Purslane Family.*

13 species

GERARDIAS The varied species of Gerardia all have dainty, showy flowers on wiry, widely branched stems, 1 to 2 feet high. The funnel-like corollas are red, purple, violet, or—rarely—white. These eastern and midland plants prefer moist habitats; one species grows in salt marshes. The False Foxgloves are taller relatives of the Gerardias, with yellow flowers and divided leaves.— *Summer to fall. Figwort Family.*

32 species

JOE-PYE WEED The tiny, lavender, and rarely white flowers of Joe-Pye weed are borne in fuzzy, flat-topped masses. The coarsely toothed leaves encircle the tall 2- to 12-foot stem. Joe-Pye weed is widespread in the East, in low ground along roadsides. Of the 50 or so related species, Boneset, with whitish flowers and paired, rough leaves, is most common.—*Late summer and fall. Composite Family.*

50 species

LOOSESTRIFES Loosestrifes are slender, colorful plants typical of Eastern marshes, moist meadows, and swamps. Several related species are aquatic. Our tallest, most showy Loosestrife has been naturalized from Europe. Several native species have smaller, pink or lavender flowers, growing in a loose spike or along the 4-sided stems. The long, toothless leaves usually grow opposite one another.— *Summer to fall. Loosestrife Family.*

16 species

MILKWEEDS   Stout-stemmed Milkweeds are tall plants that grow 2 to 5 feet high. Their broad flower clusters are red to pink, lilac, and cream-white. All parts of the plant contain a milky juice, latex, which gives Milkweed its name. Milkweeds are abundant in old fields, meadows, marshes, and moist roadsides. The seeds, with their familiar "para-chutes," sail off in the wind.—*Summer and fall. Milkweed Family.*

65 species

The following plants are covered in other sections of this book because they are predominantly of some other colors, but they include one or more species that do fit into the RED, PINK, AND MAGENTA color group:

IRONWEEDS The flowerheads of Ironweeds resemble small, dark purple Thistles, but the plants are free of spines. The leaves, long and closely toothed, are different too. Ironweeds (3 to 8 feet) grow in moist meadows and roadsides in the eastern and middle states. Some 20 species occur, all purple in color, rarely white. The best known are Tall Ironweed and New York Ironweed.—*Early fall. Composite Family.*

20 species

ASTERS Asters number some 120-150 species in the United States. Most occur in the East where, with Goldenrod, they fill spangled fields in late summer and fall. Each star-like, multipetaled flower is actually a compact cluster, called a "flowerhead." The center (disk) flowers are bright yellow; the outer (ray) flowers, often mistaken for petals, vary from blue and purple to white. When studying Asters, look at the basal leaves as well as those near the top of the plant, since they help in identification.

Asters are typical plants of open fields and roadsides, but there are woodland, swamp, and seaside species too.

They grow and spread from perennial rootstocks. Best-known Asters include the New England Aster (tall, with deep purple flowers), sometimes cultivated; the New York Aster (blue-violet flowers: thin, smooth leaves); the Heart-leaved Aster (heart-shaped leaves at the *base* of the stem, and small lilac flowers). The White Woodland Aster has a zig-zag stem, small white flowers, and smooth, heart-shaped leaves.—*Late summer to late fall. Composite Family.*

120-150 species

BLAZING-STARS These slender, handsome plants grow in dry ground along roadsides and in fields, especially in the prairies. The magenta to purple, rarely white, flower-heads are arranged compactly around the upper part of the central stalk. The narrow leaves radiate from the lower part of the stem, which grows 1 to 4 feet high, presenting a somewhat feathery appearance; hence one of its common names, Gay-feather.— *Late summer to fall. Composite Family.*

30 species

VETCHES These smooth vines, climbing by tendrils at the tip of their delicate leaves, favor cultivated fields and borders of thickets. Some 35 species, native and naturalized, are scattered throughout the United States. They make excellent fodder. Seeds and foliage are eaten by wildlife. The Common Vetch, which originated in Europe, is the most prevalent. The pea-like flowers vary from purple to blue to white.—*Late spring to fall. Pea Family.*

35 species

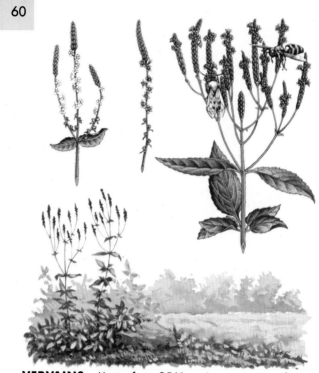

VERVAINS   Most of our 35 Vervains are native. Some are annuals; some perennials. A few have come over from Europe. Two principal types grow here. One is erect, with slender, branched spikes of small flowers; the other is a low or prostrate plant with more showy, loosely clustered flowers. Vervains vary in color from purple to blue to white and favor waste places, dry field borders, and roadsides.—*Summer to early fall. Vervain Family.*

35 species

BRODIAEAS These pretty, delicate, grassy-leaved, western wildflowers prefer meadows and sunny hillsides. Best known are the Wild Hyacinth, Firecracker Flower, and Golden Brodiaea. Their bell-shaped flowers are generally pale blue or violet (rarely yellow or crimson) and occur in loose clusters on twisted, bare stems, 6 to 20 inches high. Indians ate the small bulbs, which they called "grass nuts."—*Spring to summer. Lily Family.*

35 species

PENSTEMONS   Most of the 200 species of these showy flowers are blue, lavender, or purple, but some are red, yellow, and even white. Many are common in the West. In Colorado, Utah, and through the Rocky Mountains the Penstemons are abundant along railroad embankments and in open fields, where they merge into masses of brilliant color. Their range extends up to the rocky soils of the timberline. Only about a dozen are found in the East.

Penstemons favor moist soil, usually in open, rocky places. They grow 1 to 3 feet high, with erect stems, often

branching at the base—though the growth pattern varies. The leaves are smooth and usually opposite. The flowers are in loose clusters; each is tubular with a spreading lip. One of the common names, Beard-tongue, refers to hairy-tipped stamens that often protrude beyond the petals. Some alpine species of Penstemons are popular rock-garden plants. A large-flowered, colorful hybrid is grown in western gardens.—*Spring and summer. Figwort Family.*

200 species

VIOLETS The familiar, fragrant, delicate Violets are common in moist fields, woodlands, and roadsides in both the East and West. Four states (Ill., N. J., R. I., Wis.) have adopted the Violet as their state flower. Violets are low, leafy plants, rarely growing more than 10 inches high. The attractive flowers have 5 dainty petals, which vary in color from deep purple and blue to yellow and white. Oddly, they are usually sterile. Smaller flowers that form lower on the plant develop into small, 3-sided capsules, containing the seeds.

Not all Violets have the typical heart-shaped leaf.

Some have deeply indented, narrow leaves. The Common and Western Blue Violets, Dog Violet, and Bird-foot Violet are bluish. Of the white species, the Canada Violet is best known. The Yellow Violets appear on page 112. Over 300 species of Violets in the world have been described, and about 80 of them are found in this country. The Pansy and most cultivated Violets are descendants of wild European species, not of the eastern Field Pansy.—*Spring and early summer. Violet Family.*

80 species

HEPATICAS The inconspicuous, most familiar Hepaticas are among the first woodland harbingers of spring. They vary from lilac or bluish to white. The thick, coarse leaves are 3-lobed and last through the winter, although by spring they are discolored. Leaf and flower stems are very hairy. Hepaticas prefer the rich, leafmold soils of open woods and forest slopes. Two species grow in the East.—*Early spring. Buttercup Family.*

2 species

BLUE-CURLS These aromatic plants grow in fields and dry, open places. The western species have a stronger, less pleasant odor than the common eastern kind. The dense clusters of small flowers, with long, curling stamens, give the plant its name. The slender stems, 2 to 5 feet high, are square, like most Mints. The leaves are opposite. Blue-Curls were once used as medicine by the Indians and by early Spanish settlers.—*Summer and fall. Mint Family.*

13 species

PASQUEFLOWERS Purple, violet, and sometimes white sepals give the cup-shaped Pasqueflower its color. The flower has no petals. These low prairie plants (6 to 14 inches high) consist mainly of a cluster of dense, hairy, divided leaves—in the center of which the flower-stalk appears. After the flower is gone, silky seeds with long, feathery tails form in clusters. It is the state flower of South Dakota.— *Summer to fall. Buttercup Family.*

2 species

SELF-HEAL Self-heal, a hardy perennial of European origin, is now widely distributed in the East in open woods, fields, roadsides, and pastures. This low plant, 6 to 12 inches high, has small spikes of blue or purple flowers. Both of its common names, Self-heal and Heal-all, indicate the plant was once used medicinally— for sore throats and other minor ailments. There is only one species in this country.—*Summer. Mint Family.*

1 species

LOBELIAS Most Lobelias are blue- to purple-flow-ered. (The scarlet Cardinal Flower, a true Lobelia, page 17, is an exception.) All prefer moist ground along brooks on wet banks and in meadows. A few species grow in marsh margins, and one occurs on sandy shores, partly immersed in water. The showy flowers are arranged in loose spikes which terminate the 1- to 2-foot stem. Each flower occurs at the base of a leaf.—*Summer and fall. Blue-bell Family.*

30 species

VENUS'S-LOOKING-GLASS The small, rounded, scalloped leaves clasping the stem and enfolding the flower are field marks for this very common species. These widespread annuals of fields, gardens, and roadsides have dainty purple to blue flowers of two distinct types. The lower flowers are small and are self-pollinated. Higher up, the flowers are larger and are pollinated by bees. Plants are 1 to 2 feet high. *Summer to early fall. Bluebell Family.*

6 species

BLUE TOADFLAX This slender plant is common on dry, sandy soils, in open fields, and on dry meadows. Individually, the plants are small and frail, but in favorable situations they blanket large areas. The lavender or violet flowers have a double lip and end in a curved spur. The

1 species

minute leaves are mainly clustered at the base of the wand-like stem, 5 to 20 inches high. Blue Toadflax is a close relative of Butter-and-eggs (page 120).—*Summer to fall. Figwort Family.*

BELLFLOWERS   The delicate, bell-shaped purplish, bluish, or white flowers hang on slender, recurved stalks. The leaves grow low on the erect stem, 1 to 2 feet high. The Common Bellflower is European, but other less wide-spread and equally attractive species are native. They grow most abundantly in the East, in moist, shady fields, in marshes, and on mountain slopes. Some hardy species are cultivated. All have a bitter, milky juice.—*Summer to fall. Bluebell Family.*

25 species

NEMOPHILAS Nemophilas are low, spreading plants with scanty foliage and comparatively large, attractive saucer-shaped flowers scattered singly on slender stems. Most are native to the Pacific Coast, where about 8 species grow in meadows and on hillsides in light shade. The pale-blue to purple, 5-petaled flowers are white in the center. Some species grow under cultivation.— *Spring. Waterleaf Family.*

11 species

CHICORY A European plant, Chicory is now abundant in the United States, growing in pastures, roadsides, and waste places. The light blue flowers (rarely pinkish or white) grow close along stiff-branching stems 1 to 5 feet high. The flowers soon wither in the sunlight. Millions of pounds of Chicory root, imported or grown locally, are roasted as a coffee substitute. — *Summer and fall. Composite Family.*

1 species

BLUEBELLS Bluebells or Cowslips grow in moist, rich bottomlands, sometimes in extensive, colorful masses. The smooth, erect stem, 1 to 2 feet high, with its large floppy leaves, is topped by a loose cluster of cup-shaped flowers; these are pinkish on opening, later becoming blue or lavender. Bellflowers (page 73) are sometimes confused with Bluebells. — *Spring. Borage Family.*

20 species

BLUETS Bluets—among the daintiest and most petite of our wildflowers—grow in dry clearings, meadows, and open woods. Also called Quaker Ladies and Innocence, they are found in small colonies, making attractive patches of color. The tiny, 4-petaled flowers vary in the several species. The most common Bluet is pale bluish, nearly white, while others are generally more purple. They are pollinated by bees and small butterflies.—*Spring and summer. Madder Family.*

30 species

GENTIANS   The Gentians, usually 1 to 2 feet high, vary in appearance, color, and habitat. About 17 species grow in the West, just over half this number in the East. Flower shapes vary from a deep funnel to a shallow saucer; color, from violet to greenish blue; and habitat, from moist woods to marshes and wet meadows. All Gentians have smooth leaves, growing opposite on the stem. The flowers are in small clusters or grow individually at the ends of branches. The tiny seeds form in a thin capsule, which splits open when ripe.

The famed Fringed Gentian produces its vase-like, deeply fringed, violet-blue flower in its second year of growth. The Bottle or Closed Gentian is most common in the East. The Soapwort Gentian of the West resembles it closely. Gentian roots are used medicinally as a tonic. Some are comparatively rare within their range and should be picked with care. They are difficult to cultivate.—*Late summer and fall. Gentian Family.*

28 species

POLEMONIUMS The slender-stemmed Polemoniums (8 inches to 4 feet high) grow in cool open woods or on moist slopes, mainly in the West. The bell-shaped, funnel-like flowers have 5 petals, which fuse into a shallow tube. They range from blue to light violet and grow in loose, arched, or nodding clusters. The divided leaves alternate on the stem. The fruit is a dry capsule. One of the Polemoniums, called Jacob's Ladder, is common in the Northwest.—*Spring and summer. Phlox Family.*

12 species

CAMAS These showy plants, 1 to 2 feet high, with grasslike leaves, are known as Camas or Wild Hyacinth. They grow in rich, damp banks and moist meadows, which are sometimes blanketed by these deep blue to white flowers. Camas is closely related to the onion. Indians and early settlers relished the small, onion-like bulbs. One Indian war was caused by the white settlers' trespassing on the ceremonial Camas fields of the Nez Percé Indians.— *Spring. Lily Family.*

5 species

BLUE-EYED GRASS These starlike blue or violet flowers, with yellow centers, are borne at the top of slender, flattened stems, a foot or more high. The narrow, grasslike leaves, lying close to the stems, give the plant part of its name. Blue-eyed grass thrives in moist meadows and open places. The similar Golden-eyed grass of the Pacific coast is, of course, yellow.— *Spring and summer. Iris Family.*

40 species

PICKEREL WEEDS Pickerel weeds grow 1 to 3 feet high forming extensive beds in shallows of ponds and sluggish streams. They are often found with Arrowhead (page 150), but the Pickerel weed leaf, sometimes quite narrow, is thick and glossy, with a rounded base. The rich blue flower spike of Pickerel weed is attractive in lily ponds or outdoor aquaria. Its seeds are eaten by wild ducks.—*Summer and early fall. Pickerel weed Family.*

2 species

LUPINES Of about 130 native American species, most are confined to the West. Only one is common in the Northeast. These beautiful, finger-leaved plants abound in fields, arid plains, and deserts. Some prefer moist soil along streams. Most are 1 to 2 feet high, but some alpine Lupines are 6 inches or less. Five petals join to form the typical, delicate pea-type flowers, which grow in blue, purple, pink, white, and yellow spikes. Differently colored Lupines often grow within the same area.

The Lupine leaf usually has 5 to 7 leaflets, radiating

from a common stalk. The hard, smooth seeds, ripening in narrow, flattened pods, are a valuable food for some western gamebirds. The plants, however, are poisonous to cattle. Lupines are widely cultivated as garden flowers. The Texas state flower, the Bluebonnet, is a Lupine. Lupines and Poppies grow together in California fields and foothills, covering the ground with a mantle of blue and gold.–*Spring and summer. Pea Family.*

130 species

VIPER'S BUGLOSS Viper's Bugloss, a native of Europe, has spread over pastures, roadsides, and waste places in eastern United States. The loose spikes of tubular, showy flowers range in color from blue to purple. The closed buds are pinkish and change color as they open. The hairiness of the low, branching stems (1 to 2 feet high) and narrow leaves gives the plant a silvery-greenish appearance. It is sometimes called Blueweed.—*Summer. Borage Family.*

1 species

DAYFLOWERS About 8 very similar species of Dayflower are quite common in rich, moist soil around dwellings, along stream margins and field borders. The flower, light blue to violet, is usually set in the hollow of a heart-shaped leaf. It opens for only a few hours, on bright, warm days. The leaves are smooth, shiny, and bright green. Dayflowers grow 1 to 3 feet high on multi-branched, reclining stems.—*Early summer and fall. Spiderwort Family.*

8 species

The following plants are covered in other sections of this book because they are predominantly of some other colors, but they include one or more species that do fit into the PURPLE TO BLUE color group:

MONKEY FLOWERS Monkey flowers grow in moist places throughout the country. The one common eastern species, purplish-blue in color, favors woodlands. The more numerous western species (generally golden yellow) grow along stream margins and in mountain meadows. Over half the species are known only from California. The leaves, usually small and toothed, grow opposite on the squarish stems, 1 to 2 feet high.—*Summer and fall. Figwort Family.*

85 species

WOOD SORRELS Of about 30 species in the United States only one (Yellow Wood sorrel) is very common. It is abundant in gardens, fields, and waste places. The Violet Wood sorrel—sometimes grown as a potted plant—is a woodland species. The clover-like leaves of all Wood sorrels are divided into threes and notched at their tip. They shut at night. The plants have a pleasant, acid taste.—*Spring and summer. Wood sorrel Family.*

30 species

BUTTERFLY WEED Butterfly weed, 1 to 3 feet high, is one of the best-known and most brilliant Milkweeds (page 53). No other Milkweed has bright orange to yellow flowers in flat-topped erect clusters at the ends of the branches. Besides, Butterfly weed has a watery sap, while that of other Milkweeds is milky. The stem is usually hairy. It prefers roadside embankments and open meadows.—*Summer and early fall. Milkweed Family.*

1 species

SUNFLOWERS Of about 67 native species of Sunflowers, about 40 occur east of the Rockies. The "Russian Sunflower," an important crop plant, yielding valuable oil from its seeds, is a variety of the Common Sunflower, which may grow up to 12 feet high. The Common Sunflower is the Kansas state flower. Another, the Jerusalem Artichoke, is grown as a crop plant for its tasty, edible tubers, which are cooked and eaten like potatoes.

Most Sunflowers, 2 to 6 feet high, grow in open fields, meadows, roadsides. A few tolerate the shade in wood-

lands. They are all tall, with rough, stout stems and coarse, toothed leaves. The flowerhead is composed of many ray and disc flowers. The disc flowers vary in color and size in different species, from brown to yellow or purple. The ray flowers, usually from 10 to 25, are yellow. Wild Sunflower seeds are nutritious and are an important food for songbirds and gamebirds.—*Summer and fall. Composite Family.*

67 species

YELLOW CONEFLOWERS These Daisy-like flowers are widely distributed in fields and waste places, in dry, sandy soils over central and eastern United States. Their inverted, cone-like centers and downward-sloping rays set them off from the Sunflowers. Most Coneflowers have golden-yellow petals. An exception are the Purple Coneflowers (page 46). The conical center of Coneflowers is at first green and later becomes brown. A number of cultivated garden flowers have been developed from them.

The Black-eyed Susan or Yellow Daisy, the state flower of Maryland, is perhaps the best-known Coneflower. It has large, golden flowerheads and dark purple centers, borne on tall stems, 1 to 3 feet high. The Tall Coneflower, 3 to 10 feet high, with several large flowerheads on the branching stems, is another well-known member of this group. It prefers bottomlands or moist woods from New England south.—*Summer. Composite Family.*

17 species

TARWEEDS These are heavily-scented, sticky plants of Pacific coast fields, orchards, and dry hillsides. Most are slender, 1 to 2 feet high, occasionally up to 3 feet. The lower part of the stem has narrow leaves. The upper part is more or less branched and bears the yellowish or cream-colored flowers. The abundant Common Tarweed has large yellowish, Daisy-like "petals," ringed with red.—*Summer and fall. Composite Family.*

18 species

SNEEZEWEEDS Sneezeweeds vary in height, form, and habitat, but all have yellow flowerheads, often with a dark disk. They grow in meadows and fields. A very common southern species, Bitterweed, is a troublesome weed in upland pastures. Cows eating it during a forage scarcity give bitter-tasting milk. Two of the more attractive Sneezeweeds are cultivated.—*Summer and early fall. Composite Family.*

20 species

JEWELWEEDS Two species, also known as Touch-me-nots, grow in the East and 4 in the far West. They like moist soil and shady places and grow 1 to 5 feet high. The orange- or yellow-spurred flowers droop from slender branchlets. The ripe seed pods explode when touched,

6 species

scattering their seeds, which are eaten by several kinds of birds. The nectar of the flower is a favorite of hummingbirds, and the sap is reputed to be a treatment for poison ivy.—*Summer and early fall. Touch-me-not Family.*

DAYLILY This familiar European immigrant has spread widely. It propagates by bulbous roots and forms large colonies in fields and along roadsides. The flower stalk, 2 to 5 feet high, is topped by a number of large buds, one opening daily to become a deep orange flower. The long, linear leaves grow at its base. Among the cultivated Daylilies is an attractive, fragrant, yellow species.—*Summer. Lily Family.*

2 species

HAWKWEEDS Some 50 species of Hawkweeds, both native and naturalized from Europe, are widely distributed. They prefer dry clearings, pastures, and roadsides. The erect unbranched, hairy stem (1 to 3 feet high) bears yellow, orange, or reddish flowerheads at the top. At the base is a rosette of hairy leaves. The attractive Rattlesnake weed is a Hawkweed of open, eastern woodlands.—*Summer to early fall. Composite Family.*

50 species

BUTTERCUPS   There are about 60 species of Buttercups in the United States, distributed widely in low moist places, meadows, and marshes. A few even grow submerged in water. Some are creepers, but most are erect and branching. They all have shiny, "varnished," butter-yellow petals (occasionally white), enclosing numerous stamens. The Bulb Buttercup has adapted itself to lawns and meadows.—*Spring to fall. Buttercup Family.*

60 species

CALIFORNIA POPPY The California Poppy, state flower of California, is one of the best-known western flowers. It is abundant in valleys and foothills of the Pacific coast and in parts of the Rockies, covering large areas with orange-golden flowers, which open during the day. It is also cultivated in horticultural forms that vary in color to pink, cream, or white.—*Spring. Poppy Family.*

9 species

DANDELIONS These common European weeds have spread to nearly every lawn. However, they offer some compensation. Their roots contain a drug used in treating the liver. The leaves, very rich in vitamins, are prized for spring salads, and wine is made from the flowers. The native western Dandelions are also "honey" plants. Their seeds are eaten extensively by birds.—*Spring to fall. Composite Family.*

9 species

GOLDENRODS About 100 species of Goldenrods grow in this country. All of them are native and most are found in the East. While Goldenrods are easy to recognize, species identification is difficult. Note the form of the basal leaves if you want to be sure *what* Goldenrod you have found. Goldenrods prefer open locations in meadows and fields and along roadsides. A few are adapted to marshes, sandy beaches, deserts, and mountains. In the East, where they cover acre after acre in the fall, Goldenrods are very impressive. As a cause of hay fever, they are not as obnoxious as is generally believed. The Ragweeds cause pollen-sensitive people much more suffering than do Goldenrods.

Goldenrods are generally 2 to 4 feet high, though some occasionally grow twice that high. The stem is often stout, branching considerably near the top. The tiny flower clusters range from deep yellow in the Showy and Seaside Goldenrods to paler yellows and creamy white in the Silverrod or White Goldenrod. Many kinds are hairy and coarse; others, like the Slender and Lance-leaved

Goldenrods, are delicate. Goldenrods usually have a pungent odor, but several are pleasingly fragrant and one, Sweet Goldenrod, is anise-scented. The leaves of this species have been dried and used locally as a tea or tonic. Try it; it is common throughout the East. Goldenrod is the state flower of Kentucky and Nebraska.—*Summer and fall. Composite Family.*

100 species

RABBITBRUSHES These resinous western plants, with their masses of small yellow flowers in flattish clusters, may be mistaken for Goldenrod, a near relative. The leaves are narrow and elongated. Rabbitbrushes grow in shrubby clumps, about 3 feet high. About 12 species make up a large part of the vegetation of our arid plains, furnishing food and cover for rabbits, deer and antelope, and other wildlife.— *Summer and fall. Composite Family.*

12 species

STICK-TIGHTS Stick-tights are common. Their familiar brown, pronged seeds attach themselves to your clothing during a walk in fields or along roadsides. The plants are erect and branched, 2 to 3 feet high. The flowerheads consist of many tubular florets—yellow, brownish-yellow, or green—usually with a series of petal-like, yellow ray flowers along the outer margin. Beggar-ticks and Bur Marigolds belong here.—*Summer and fall. Composite Family.*

25 species

ST.-JOHN'S-WORTS Some of these common plants, with bright, varied-sized yellow flowers, have come to us from Asia by way of Europe. They grow 4 inches to 6 feet tall along roadsides, in moist, open lands, and even above the timberline. The erect stems sometimes branch very much near the top. The leaves grow opposite, clasping the stem. Some are spotted with tiny, transparent dots.—*Summer and early fall. St.-John's-wort Family.*

41 species

YELLOW CLOVERS The yellow-flowered Hop and Bur Clovers are related to the red, pink, and white species (pages 24-25). These low plants, only a few inches high, grow in lawns, orchards, fields, and roadsides. The 3 Hop Clovers have tiny, compact flowerheads. Bur Clover has only 2 to 5 flowers in a cluster, which matures into coiled, bur-like seed pods with tiny curved hooks. —*Spring and early summer. Pea Family.*

5 species

ADDER'S-TONGUES The delightful Adder's-tongues are low plants, 5 to 10 inches high, of moist woodlands and mountains. The pair of mottled leaves, with a nodding, 6 parted flower—yellow, violet, or white—rising on a short stalk between them, is characteristic. Adder's-tongues grow from small bulbs, which are edible when cooked. Western species are also known as Avalanche Lilies.—*Spring. Lily Family.*

18 species

YELLOW ORCHIDS These Yellow Orchids belong with the well-known species on pages 36-37. The Yellow Lady-Slipper is widespread in rich, moist woodlands. The Yellow-fringed Orchids bear small clusters of feathery, orange flowers on erect stalks. Though quite different from the Lady-Slipper, they too have all the grace and rare beauty of the Orchid Family. Fringed Orchids are also white, pink and purple.—*Spring and summer. Orchid Family.*

YELLOW VIOLETS These include one of the tallest of the Violets (Downy Yellow Violet, 6 to 18 inches high). All Yellow Violets have heart-shaped leaves and the typical violet flower borne on rather short stems. Flowers are a pale to light yellow, sometimes streaked with brown or purple. Hairy stems and leaves mark the Downy Yellow Violet. The smooth Yellow Violet has more leaves than the Downy Yellow.— *Spring. Violet Family.*

10 species

EVENING PRIMROSES   Some Evening Primroses open in the late afternoon (as their name implies) and close the next morning. The flowers vary in size from moderate to large and, though generally pure yellow, range to pink or white in some species. The plants usually have a rosette of toothed leaves and, in a few species, there is no erect stem. In others, the stems are 1 to 4 feet high. —*Summer and early fall. Evening Primrose Family.*

50 species

GROUNDSELS About 100 native species of Senecio, known as Groundsel, Ragwort, and Squaw-weed, usually grow on the open plains. They are herbs, with yellow flowers in flat-topped clusters at the ends of stems, something like those of a Yellow Aster. Some have simple, erect stems. Others branch at the base or above. The leaves alternate on the stem—some hairy, some pointed, some divided into narrow lobes.—*Summer, fall, and winter. Composite Family.*

100 species

FALSE FOXGLOVES These erect, branched plants, 2 to 4 feet tall, grow in open eastern woodlands. The 10 species all have large, showy, yellow, tubular, 5-petaled flowers. Leaves are opposite; some are finely divided. The seeds of some species are winged. False Foxgloves are root parasites. They become attached to roots of trees and so gain part of their nourishment. The Gerardias (page 50) with purple flowers are close relatives.—*Late summer to early fall. Figwort Family.*

10 species

WINTER CRESS The 4-petaled flowers show that these plants belong with the many species of European and native Mustards. Other Mustards also have yellow flowers in small clusters. Winter cress or Yellow Rocket is cultivated abroad as a salad plant. The smooth stem, 1 to 2 feet high, bears cut and lobed leaves. The seed pods are 4-angled; 1 to 3 inches long.—*Spring and summer. Mustard Family.*

3 species

CINQUEFOILS The shiny golden Cinquefoils, or Five-fingers, brighten pastures, meadows, hills, and road-sides. Common species are creepers, though a number grow erect or even shrub-like, 1 to 3 feet high. The toothed, strawberry-like leaves are 3- or 5-lobed. There are about 75 species of Cinquefoil, mostly in cooler areas. Flowers, besides yellow, are white, red, and purple.—*Summer and early fall. Rose Family.*

75 species

MULLEINS Great Mullein is a very common European plant of roadsides, fields, and dry waste places. The flower stalk is a stout, erect candelabra, 2 to 7 feet tall, with a basal rosette of large soft, hairy leaves. The 5-petaled, light yellow flowers open a few at a time, in a branched spike. The smaller Moth Mullein is more slender, with smooth leaves and yellow, white, or pink flowers.—*Summer and fall. Figwort Family.*

5 species

PARTRIDGE PEAS These semitropical plants have fern-like leaves and golden yellow flowers. About 30 species occur, most of them in the South in fields, roadsides, and waste places. They are also known as Sensitive Plants and Bee-blossom. The delicate, compound leaves, controlled by an unusual mechanism, fold slowly when touched. The hard seeds are eaten by quail.—*Summer and fall. Pea Family.*

30 species

BUTTER-AND-EGGS Butter-and-eggs, originally from Europe, has spread over northern fields, pastures, road-sides, and city lots. The erect stems, 6 to 30 inches high, are topped by yellow and orange 2-lipped flowers, spurred at the base. Were these very bright, attractive flowers rarer, they would arouse greater admiration. The leaves are narrow, alternate, and gray-green in color.—*Summer and early fall. Figwort Family.*

1 species

BELLWORTS These graceful plants grow from underground stems in rich woods and bottomlands. The nodding, straw-colored or lemon-yellow, bell-shaped flowers hang from the slender stem, which is 6 to 18 inches high. Below the flowers are lance-shaped leaves, which in one of the two common eastern species are pierced by the stem. The seeds are in a 3-parted capsule.—*Spring and early summer. Lily Family.*

5 species

CREAMCUPS   This western flower grows in moist fields, meadows, and hillsides. It is especially abundant along the Pacific coast, where it may cover entire fields. As its name implies, this plant has creamy-yellow, 6-petaled cup-like flowers, borne on thin, leafless stalks. Creamcups are low plants with narrow, hairy leaves. The seeds develop in narrow, poppy-like pods. — *Spring. Poppy Family.*

1 species

ERIOGONUMS   Most of this large western group of about 150 species have widely branched, umbrella-like clusters of small, yellow, white, pink, or orange-red flowers. The small leaves are usually confined to a basal rosette around the leafless stem, 1 to 3 feet high. These plants favor dry plains and plateaus. A desert species with an inflated stem is known as Desert Trumpet.—*Spring to early summer. Buckwheat Family.*

150 species

The following plants are covered in other sections of this book because they are predominantly of some other colors, but they include one or more species that do fit into the ORANGE TO YELLOW color group:

MARIPOSAS These graceful white, yellow, and lilac flowers, up to 1 foot high, grow in meadows and hillsides. They are common, often blanketing desert foothills in the spring. The tulip-like flower, slender stem, and grasslike leaves are characteristic, as are the small edible bulbs, used by the Indians. They are known also as Mariposa lily, Mariposa Tulip, or Sego lily. The latter, a white species, is the Utah state flower.—*Spring and summer. Lily Family.*

50 species

DUTCHMAN'S-BREECHES This is a fragrant, attractive plant of rich eastern woods, often found with Spring Beauty and Yellow Adder's-tongue. The 4 to 8 cream to pink flowers hang on a slender stalk 6 to 12 inches high, their double-spurred corolla stained with yellow. The

leaves are almost fern-like. Another species, Squirrel Corn, has a single-spurred flower, similar to that of the western Bleeding-heart.—*Spring. Fumitory Family.*

1 species

MEADOW RUES These tall (1 to 7 feet), stately plants prefer meadows, rich woodland borders, and other moist, open places. There are several species; those of the West are smaller than the eastern ones. In summer the upper part of the plant is covered with masses of small white or greenish-white star-like flowers. The leaves, daintily divided into sub-groups of 3 leaflets, make the plants even more attractive.—*Summer to early fall. Buttercup Family.*

15 species

RUE ANEMONE This is a low (5 to 12 inches), delicate woodland plant with attractive compound leaves. Its flowers, arranged in clusters of 2 or 3 on a slender stalk, are usually white, sometimes tinged with pink. The small, rounded, deep-green leaves are long-stemmed and are divided into groups of 3, resembling the foliage of the Meadow rue. Rue Anemone is common in open woods.—*Spring. Buttercup Family.*

1 species

BUGBANES These tall herbs, 4 to 6 feet high, of rich, open woodlands go under such names as Cohosh, Black Snakeroot, and Fairy-candles. The tiny, white, feathery blooms branch in spire-like clusters. Their unpleasant stale odor attracts flies, which pollinate the plant. The large, compound leaves are divided into sharply-toothed leaflets. The fruit is a many-seeded, purple capsule.—*Summer. Buttercup Family.*

6 species

SAXIFRAGES Most Saxifrages have mats of toothed, rounded leaves, growing at the base of bare, erect flower stalks, 2 to 15 inches high. They are often hairy or sticky. The small white to greenish flowers are 5-petaled, in flattish clusters. Many Saxifrages are northern plants of moist meadows and mountain slopes. Some are common in eastern woodlands. The roots were used as medicine.—*Spring and summer. Saxifrage Family.*

50 species

BUNCHBERRY   The flowers of Bunchberry, also known as Dwarf Cornel, resemble those of flowering Dogwood— and with good reason, for the plants are close relatives. The 4 greenish-white "petals," set over a whorl of 4 to 6 leaves, are actually bracts surrounding a cluster of tiny, green- or yellow-petaled flowers. The unusual symmetry of the plant sets it off from all others. Bunchberry grows in cool northern woods, where it is partial to rich, acid soils. In fall the short stems, 2 to 8 inches high, are topped by clusters of scarlet berries, which give this attractive plant its name. — *Spring and summer. Dogwood Family.*

1 species

FOAMFLOWERS Note the small, hairy, maple-like leaves which grow close to the ground. The flower stalk, often a foot high, bears a loose spike of fine, erect, white flowers with long orange stamens. These plants of rich northern woods are very similar to the smaller, more delicate Mitreworts, one of which has a pair of small leaves halfway up the flower stalk. Mitreworts are also woodland plants. —*Spring to early summer. Saxifrage Family.*

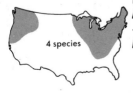

4 species

WINTERGREENS Wintergreens are woodland plants, often growing in the shade of evergreens. The small, shiny, deep-green leaves on very low stems, 2 to 5 inches high, remain on the plant all winter. When crushed, they exude the familiar wintergreen fragrance. The small, white tubular flowers mature into aromatic red berries, which gamebirds eat. Salal, a western species, is larger and shrub-like.—*Summer. Heath Family.*

4 species

SOLOMON'S-SEAL   The greenish bell-shaped flowers of Solomon's-seal hang along the slender stalk. But the small, starry, white flowers of Spikenard or False Solomon's-seal form a terminal cluster. Several species of Solomon's-seal and Spikenard favor open northern woods. The flowers of Solomon's-seal ripen into plump, blue berries; the Spikenard, into smaller bronze or reddish berries.—*Spring and early summer. Lily Family.*

8 species

CANADA MAYFLOWER   This tiny, common plant that carpets northern forests has a cluster of small white flowers at its tip. It is also known as Massachusetts Mayflower and False Lily-of-the-valley. The shiny leaves are broad and heart-shaped at the base. Only 2 or 3 of them grow on the short stem, which is 4 to 6 inches high. The flowers ripen into spotted, greenish white berries, turning to dull red in the fall.—*Summer. Lily Family.*

2 species

PIPSISSEWAS Common in deep, well-drained woods, Pipsissewas are widespread across the Northern states and in mountain areas. The waxy white or pinkish flowers, 5-petaled and quite fragrant, occur in a group of 3 or 4 at the top of the short, naked stalk. The narrow, leathery leaves, 1 to 3 inches long, are strongly toothed. In one eastern species the leaves are mottled by light markings along the midveins.—*Summer. Wintergreen Family.*

3 species

CHICKWEEDS Of about 25 kinds of Chickweeds, native and naturalized, only one, the Common Chickweed, is widespread and well known. It is a small, weedy plant of gardens, fields, and moist places. The weak, reclining stems, often a foot long, bear pairs of small oval leaves. The flowers have deeply notched white petals and develop into papery capsules, containing small seeds that songbirds relish.—*Spring. Pink Family.*

25 species

YARROWS These aromatic, lacy-leaved, grayish-green plants are topped with a flat head of small, dull-white (occasionally purple) flowers. The common Yarrow or Milfoil is a typical roadside weed, growing 1 to 2 feet high in meadows and fields. Aromatic Yarrow was once used for colds and as a tonic. Several western species include a smaller alpine relative and one with a woolly stem.— Summer and fall. Composite Family.

5 species

QUEEN-ANNE'S-LACE The flat-topped, lacy, dull-white flower clusters often have a single dark purple flower in the center. The leaves are finely divided. This coarse weed thrives in cultivated fields and exposed grounds. It is particularly abundant in the Northeast, where it has spread widely. Queen-Anne's-lace or Wild Carrot is one of the worst European weeds. A smaller, less common species occurs in the West.—*Summer and early fall. Parsley Family.*

2 species

BEDSTRAWS Bedstraws are common herbs of open woods and moist fields. They vary in form and habit, but all are small and rather delicate plants, 1 to 2 feet high. Their slender stems are often weak and reclining. A few are covered with rasping hairs. The tiny, 4-parted white

65 species

or yellow flowers are grouped either at the base of the leaf or at the top of the plant. The narrow leaves are in pairs or whorls of 4 to 6.—*Summer. Madder Family.*

GROMWELLS These are rough-haired, slender plants, common in most western fields and roadsides. Their small white, yellow, or orange flowers top the plant in curved clusters. Except for color, the Gromwells' flowers and hairy foliage resemble Forget-me-nots, related blue-flowered plants. The seeds are white and stony. The roots were used by Indians in making a purple dye.—*Summer and early fall. Borage Family.*

15 species

SWEET CLOVERS Despite the name, Sweet clovers are not true Clovers. These widespread plants are of foreign origin. They are generally more abundant in the West, where they grow along highways and in waste places. Sweet clovers are raised locally as a forage crop and produce fine honey. The bushy plants, 2 to 5 feet high, have sprays of tiny aromatic flowers, cream-white to golden yellow. White is commonest.—*Summer. Pea Family.*

3 species

FIELD DAISY The Field Daisy is beautiful and abundant in eastern fields and roadsides. The plants, 1 to 2 feet high, grow in clumps, topped by white-rayed, yellow-centered flowerheads. Most of the toothed leaves cluster at the base of the stem. Cultivated Chrysanthemums and Daisies are relatives of the Field Daisy; so is Feverfew, a branching species with smaller flowers and leaves.—*Summer and early fall. Composite Family.*

1 species

MAYWEEDS   Several similar Daisy-like plants naturalized from Europe have spread through the West, where they are found in barnyards, fields, waste places, and roadsides. Birds occasionally eat their seeds. Mayweeds are common in the East also. The common species grows

4 species

6 to 18 inches high. Its feathery leaves have a pungent, rotting odor. Camomile tea is made from the flowers. —*Summer and fall. Composite Family.*

PARTRIDGEBERRY   This slender, evergreen creeper takes root along its prostrate stem. The small, shiny, oval leaves are white-veined and grow in opposite pairs. The cream-white or pale pink flowers are 4-petaled. The petals are united to form a miniature tube. The flowers are in pairs, too. Each pair eventu-ally forms the aromatic, red part-ridgeberry or twinberry, eaten by birds.—*Spring to early summer. Madder Family.*

1 species

TOOTHWORTS These slender plants thrive in moist woods and along streams. The flowers, medium small, white or pinkish, grow in clusters. Their 4 petals are somewhat cross-shaped. The smooth stems, 6 to 15 inches high, bear toothed leaves. The edible, peppery root tastes like Watercress. A western species is also abundant, and meadows in the coast ranges are whitened when it blooms. —*Spring. Mustard Family.*

8 species

MAYAPPLE Large colonies of Mayapple grow in moist southeastern woods. The single, medium-large white flower is at the junction of the pair of large, umbrella-like leaves. The edible lemon-yellow fruit has a strawberry flavor, but the root, stem, and leaves are poisonous. During the Middle Ages, Mayapple, also known as Mandrake, was prized because of its supposed magic properties.—*Late spring. Barberry Family.*

1 species

POKEWEEDS These tall plants, 4 to 12 feet high, are common in fallow fields and waste places. The small, whitish flowers, sometimes tinged with purple, grow in clusters. The dark purple berries have earned for the plants the names Inkberry and Pokeberry. Birds eat the berries and may become intoxicated from them. The young shoots are edible when cooked, but the large root is poisonous.—*Fall. Poke-weed Family.*

2 species

BLOODROOT The Bloodroot—a first sign of spring in the Northeast—has a beautiful, fragile flower. The clear, white, long petals radiate from the golden yellow center. They close in the evening. The single, irregular leaf wraps around the flower stalk. The plant has a milky, acrid, orange sap. Bloodroot is common along shaded roadsides and in rich woods, growing to a height of 10 inches.—*Early spring. Poppy Family.*

1 species

ARROWHEADS Arrowheads are marsh and aquatic plants that thrive along ponds and margins of sluggish streams. Pure white, 3-petaled, Lily-like flowers are borne in a spire 1 to 2 feet above the cluster of arrow-shaped leaves. (In a few species the leaves are not arrow-shaped.)

16 species

Algonquin Indians roasted the underground tubers, as did the early settlers. Ducks also find them a palatable food. — *Summer and early fall. Water Plantain Family.*

PRICKLY POPPIES Over a half dozen species of these bushy plants grow in dry places in the West, where they are also known as Mexican poppy and Thistle-poppy. The showy, large white or yellow blooms are borne singly at the ends of branched stalks. The leaves and stems of the plants, 2 to 3 feet high, are covered with sharp prickles. They have a bitter, yellow juice. The seed pod is an oblong capsule full of shotlike, round seeds.—*Summer. Poppy Family.*

13 species

The following plants are covered in other sections of this book because they are predominantly of some other colors, but they include one or more species that do fit into the CREAM TO WHITE color group:

SCIENTIFIC NAMES

The plants in this book are presented mainly in groups (or genera); the scientific name of each genus illustrated is given below. If more than one genus is represented on a page, we identify them from left to right. When a single species of wildflower is treated separately, its full scientific name is given: the genus name is first, then the specific name (the two together denote the species).

INDEX

MEASURING SCALE (IN MILLIMETERS AND CENTIMETERS)

MEASURING SCALE (IN INCHES)

RECORDS